Tipper Gore

The People to Know Series

Neil Armstrong
*The First Man
on the Moon*
0-89490-828-6

Isaac Asimov
Master of Science Fiction
0-7660-1031-7

Bill Clinton
United States President
0-89490-437-X

Hillary Rodham Clinton
Activist First Lady
0-89490-583-X

Bill Cosby
Actor and Comedian
0-89490-548-1

Willa Cather
Writer of the Prairie
0-89490-980-0

Walt Disney
Creator of Mickey Mouse
0-89490-694-1

Bob Dole
Legendary Senator
0-89490-825-1

Marian Wright Edelman
*Fighting for
Children's Rights*
0-89490-623-2

Bill Gates
*Billionaire
Computer Genius*
0-89490-824-3

Jane Goodall
*Protector of
Chimpanzees*
0-89490-827-8

Al Gore
*United States
Vice President*
0-89490-496-5

Tipper Gore
*Activist, Author,
Photographer*
0-7660-1142-9

Ernest Hemingway
Writer and Adventurer
0-89490-979-7

Ron Howard
*Child Star &
Hollywood Director*
0-89490-981-9

John F. Kennedy
*President of the
New Frontier*
0-89490-693-3

John Lennon
*The Beatles
and Beyond*
0-89490-702-6

Jack London
*A Writer's
Adventurous Life*
0-7660-1144-5

Maya Lin
Architect and Artist
0-89490-499-X

Barbara McClintock
*Nobel Prize
Geneticist*
0-89490-983-5

Christopher Reeve
*Hollywood's Man
of Courage*
0-7660-1149-6

Ann Richards
*Politician, Feminist,
Survivor*
0-89490-497-3

Sally Ride
*First American Woman
in Space*
0-89490-829-4

Will Rogers
Cowboy Philosopher
0-89490-695-X

Franklin D. Roosevelt
*The Four-Term
President*
0-89490-696-8

Steven Spielberg
*Hollywood
Filmmaker*
0-89490-697-6

Martha Stewart
*Successful
Businesswoman*
0-89490-984-3

Amy Tan
*Author of
The Joy Luck Club*
0-89490-699-2

Alice Walker
*Author of
The Color Purple*
0-89490-620-8

Simon Wiesenthal
*Tracking Down
Nazi Criminals*
0-89490-830-8

Frank Lloyd Wright
Visionary Architect
0-7660-1032-5

People to Know

Tipper Gore

Activist, Author, Photographer

Barbara Kramer

Enslow Publishers, Inc.

44 Fadem Road PO Box 38
Box 699 Aldershot
Springfield, NJ 07081 Hants GU12 6BP
USA UK

http://www.enslow.com

Library of Congress Cataloging-in-Publication Data

Kramer, Barbara.
    Tipper Gore : activist, author, photographer / by Barbara Kramer.
        p. cm. — (People to Know)
    Summary: Chronicles the political and personal life of the wife of Vice President
Al Gore, focusing on her work with the Parents Music Resource Center and the
National Mental Health Association, the books she has written, and her duties as
"Second Lady" of the United States.
    ISBN 0-7660-1142-9
    1. Gore, Tipper, 1948– . —Juvenile literature. 2. Vice-Presidents' spouses—
United States—Biography—Juvenile literature. 3. Gore, Albert, 1948– . —Juvenile
literature. [1. Gore, Tipper, 1948– . 2. Vice-Presidents' wives.] I. Title.
II. Series.
E840.8.G66K73 1999
973.929'092—dc21

   [B]   98-26888
                                                    CIP
                                                      AC

Printed in the United States of America

10 9 8 7 6 5 4 3 2 1

To Our Readers:
All Internet addresses in this book were active and appropriate when we went to press.
Any comments or suggestions can be sent by e-mail to Comments@enslow.com or to
the address on the back cover.

Illustration Credits: AP/Wide World Photos, pp. 27, 46, 57, 62; Arnie
Sachs/Consolidated News Pictures/Archive Photos, p. 53; The White House,
p. 6; Dennis Brack/Consolidated News Pictures/Archive Photos, pp. 68, 72;
Jose R. Lopez/New York Times Co./Archive Photos, pp. 10, 41; Kirsten
Bremmer/New York Times Co./Archive Photos, p. 83; Lee Romero/New York
Times Co./Archive Photos, p. 66; Nancy Rhoda, pp. 33, 36, 49; Reuters/Jeff
Christensen/Archive Photos, p. 94; Reuters/Novovtich/Archive Photos, p. 89;
Reuters/Scott Olsen/Archive Photos, p. 97; Ron Sachs/Consolidated News
Pictures/Archive Photos, p. 77; St. Agnes School, pp. 15, 19.

Cover Credit: Callie Shell, White House photographer

Contents

Mary Elizabeth "Tipper" Gore

"An American Reunion"

It was January 17, 1993, and Tipper Gore was boarding a bus in Charlottesville, Virginia. It was one in a caravan of buses headed for Washington, D.C., for the presidential inauguration. In three days, Bill Clinton, a Democrat, would be sworn in as president of the United States. Tipper Gore's husband, Albert Gore, Jr., would become vice president.

The Gores and Clintons had begun the morning with a tour of Monticello, the home of former president Thomas Jefferson. Now they would follow the same route that Jefferson had traveled on his way to the White House in 1801.

The bus brought back memories for Tipper Gore. During the presidential campaign, the Clintons and

Gores had traveled across the United States in a bus caravan. Other candidates flew from stop to stop, but Bill Clinton wanted a chance to get out and meet the people. Tipper Gore agreed: "I didn't want to spend all my time shaking hands with people I already knew."[1]

She had said that she wanted the campaign to be fun, and for her, it appeared that it was. She laughed freely as she shook hands with voters. One minute she was waving to a cheering crowd of people, and the next minute she was photographing them. Gore, who is a professional photographer, wanted to capture the events of the campaign on film.

Secret Service agents gave Gore the code name "Skylark." A skylark is a type of bird, but it also means someone who frolics, a prankster or a person who likes to have a good time. Gore appeared to be living up to her code name one day during the campaign when she sprayed reporters with a water pistol.

Now that the campaign was over, the Clintons and Gores headed to Washington, D.C., for the celebration. All along the one-hundred-twenty-mile route, people came out to greet them. They cheered and waved American flags. It was a happy time for Tipper Gore, who had not always enjoyed this kind of public support.

In 1985, she had started a campaign for warning labels to be put on records that contained violent or sexually explicit lyrics. She was not prepared for the angry response she got from the people who disagreed with her. Several rock singers recorded songs that made fun of her. Music fans, who said she hated rock music, booed her. Reporters created a cartoonlike image of her as a bored, uptight housewife who hated sex.

People who knew Gore said she was nothing like that. Her friends described her as funny, down-to-earth, honest, and friendly. "I just don't even recognize the person I've been reading about," one of her friends noted.[2]

Public opinion about Gore had changed since then. By 1992, a voluntary labeling system for records had been in effect for several years. A similar system for television was being considered. People were now talking about family values, and the Republicans had made it a campaign issue. It now appeared that Gore had been ahead of her time.

Today she heard only cheers as the bus pulled into Washington, D.C. At the Lincoln Memorial, more than three hundred thousand people lined both sides of the Reflecting Pool. Trumpets played as president-elect Bill Clinton, his wife, Hillary, and Al and Tipper Gore walked down the steps of the Memorial. Overhead, twenty-one jets flew in formation.

For the next couple of hours, the people were entertained by a variety of musicians, including Kenny Rogers, Aretha Franklin, and rapper LL Cool J. Then the Gores joined hands to walk with the Clintons in a procession across Memorial Bridge. "The force of the crowd, surging forward to see us and touch us, was like a tidal wave advancing," Tipper Gore later wrote.[3]

They made their way to Lady Bird Johnson Park for the "Bells of Hope" ceremony. It began at 6:00 P.M. when Bill Clinton rang a replica of the Liberty Bell.

President-elect Bill Clinton rings a replica of the Liberty Bell with the help of Hillary Clinton and Albert Gore III. To the right are Tipper Gore, Vice President–elect Al Gore, Jr., and their daughter Kristin.

People all across the United States also rang bells, and the astronauts aboard the space shuttle *Endeavor* rang a bell in space. Minutes later, fireworks exploded. This was a planned show of support for the soon-to-be president and vice president.

The day's activities were the beginning of a week-long celebration called "An American Reunion." For Tipper Gore, it was a joyful homecoming. She was born in Washington, D.C., on August 19, 1948. She had grown up only a few miles from the White House and had learned to drive in the Pentagon parking lot. She never imagined then that one day she would become an advisor to the president of the United States.

Sports, Pranks, and Teenage Rebellion

She was named Mary Elizabeth Aitcheson, but most people just called her Tipper. It was a nickname her mother gave her when she was a baby. "I guess she thought that Mary Elizabeth was too grand for a little girl," Gore later said.[1] The nickname came from an old Spanish ballad called "Tippy Tippy Tin." It was a tune Tipper's mother sang to her little daughter.

Tipper's parents were Jack and Margaret Aitcheson. It was a second marriage for the former Margaret Carlson. Her first marriage was to Alfred Odom in 1942. Carlson was only seventeen at the time. Her young husband, a soldier, was later killed in World War II.

Carlson married Jack Aitcheson in 1947. Their

daughter, Tipper, was born the next year. Tipper's parents separated in 1949, though they were not divorced until 1952. Tipper and her mother moved in with Tipper's grandparents in Arlington, Virginia.

They lived in a redbrick Tudor-style home that had been built by Tipper's grandfather in 1938. Divorce was not common in the 1950s, and not many mothers had jobs outside their home. Tipper was sometimes teased at school because she did not have a father living at home. She was also the only one in the neighborhood whose mother worked full-time. As a result, she sometimes felt like an outsider among her classmates.

Although some reports have said that Tipper did not have much of a relationship with her father, she disagrees. He lived nearby and she saw him on Sundays and more often during school vacations. It was the best she could expect at a time when divorce arrangements were very different from what is common today. "Mothers traditionally got custody, and dads got visitation rights, not joint custody," Gore has noted.[2]

Jack Aitcheson later married a woman who had three children from a previous marriage. One of the daughters was about Tipper's age. Aitcheson eventually divorced his second wife and remarried, this time to a woman who had three sons. Although Tipper spent time with her half brothers and half sisters, it was not the same as living under the same roof. Gore has often said that she was lonely as an only child and that she envied her friends who had brothers and sisters at home.

Tipper spent a lot of time outdoors as a child. "I was a tomboy, always outside," she says.[3] She liked to climb trees and play in her tree house. She had a pet parakeet, played with tree frogs, and even collected tadpoles.

She also enjoyed reading. She and her friends organized a book club. They put all their books together and then checked them out as if they were running a library.

Tipper had a religious upbringing. She went to Sunday school each week and attended St. Agnes Episcopal School in Alexandria, Virginia. At that time it was an all-girls school, but it has since merged with a boys school. Her favorite subject was history.

She was a popular student and a bit mischievous. One of her pranks was to spread clear plastic wrap across the top of an open toilet bowl. With the toilet seat down, an unsuspecting person would not see the plastic wrap until it was too late. It created a real mess when someone actually tried to use the toilet.

Tipper was also athletic and participated in a variety of sports. She was on the softball team, played basketball, and was captain of the field hockey team. She and one of her friends were the badminton champions at their school.

Sometimes Tipper's mother had to work and could not attend her daughter's school activities. Gore says she does not recall feeling upset by that. "I remember appreciating her, at times realizing why she was working and what it meant to me," Gore said.[4] That did not mean that she and her mother always saw eye-to-eye.

Tipper was active in sports and was captain of her field hockey team. In this team photo she is in the second row the sixth from the left.

Gore says she went through a normal teenage rebellious stage and recalled having a few arguments with her mother. "The angriest time I ever had was when I was fourteen," Gore told a reporter. "She took all the phones in the house and locked them in the car trunk."[5] Their disagreement was over the amount of time Tipper was spending talking on the phone. Tipper would rather talk on the phone to her friends than study. Her mother thought Tipper needed to spend less time on the phone.

Tipper got a set of drums when she was fourteen and taught herself to play. One of her favorite groups was the Beatles. She would put one of their records, or Sandy Nelson's "Let There Be Drums," on the stereo and play along. After a year of practice, she and some of her friends formed an all-girls band. "It was basically three guitars and drums and a girl who really sang well," Gore later explained.[6]

They called themselves the Wildcats. The name came from Tipper's mother's car, a black Buick Wildcat. The band usually practiced at Tipper's house because it was too much trouble to haul around a set of drums. They had a few local gigs, including the St. Agnes Spring Festival and an appearance at a Democratic rally.

Some of the staff at Gore's school did not think the band was a good idea. "Our headmistress, Miss McBride, did not approve of my playing the drums. She didn't think it was ladylike," Gore recalled.[7]

When Tipper was sixteen, she attended a graduation dance at St. Albans Episcopal School for Boys in Washington, D.C. There she met seventeen-year-old Al Gore, Jr. Although they had both arrived with other dates, she was attracted to him immediately. "I thought he was sexy, serious, smart, and funny. Funny is real important with me, a sense of humor helps you get through life," she later said.[8]

Tipper knew that Al Gore was attracted to her, too. She was not surprised when he called the next day and asked her for a date.[9]

Al Gore, Jr., was the son of Albert Gore, Sr., who was a powerful Democratic senator from Tennessee. By the time Al, Jr., was born in 1948, his father had already served ten years in the House of Representatives. He spent fourteen years in the House and was then elected to the Senate when Al Jr. was four years old.

Al Gore's mother, Pauline, was one of the first women to graduate from Vanderbilt Law School in

Nashville. The Gores had one other child, Nancy, who was ten years older than Al.

The family divided their time between their farm near Carthage, Tennessee, and their residence on the eighth floor of the Fairfax Hotel in Washington, D.C. Al, Jr., lived in Washington, D.C., during the school year. He spent summers, Christmases, and other school vacations in Carthage. "I've always lived in two places, two lives," he later said.[10]

Al and Tipper saw each other often that summer, and Al Gore broke off a longtime relationship with a girl from Carthage. That fall, he began college at Harvard University in Cambridge, Massachusetts. He wanted to be a writer, so he majored in English. He later changed his major to government, but he still planned to be a writer someday.

He and Tipper kept in touch, and Al encouraged her to attend a college near Harvard after she graduated from high school. Over spring break, Tipper made a trip to Boston to visit colleges in the area. Her grandmother went along as a chaperone.

Tipper graduated from high school a year later, in 1966. That fall she began classes in Boston at Garland College, a two-year school. (Garland College is now part of Simmons College.) It was a stepping-stone between her small high school and a large university. "I was educated at an Episcopal girls school, so I felt I was not ready for a huge school right away," she said.[11]

Gore had hoped to drop the nickname Tipper when she got to college, but when her old friends telephoned, they asked for Tipper. No one knew whom to call to the phone until Gore confessed that the nickname belonged to her. Soon her new college friends were also calling her Tipper.

In 1967, she visited the Gore farm in Carthage for the first time. Knowing her love of animals, Al Gore had arranged a special surprise for her. He had found a baby skunk on the farm and had taken it to a veterinarian to have its scent glands removed. He and his sister bathed the skunk, and when Tipper arrived, he gave it to her.

She was happy with her new pet, which she named Mandy. Pauline Gore provided a cardboard box to use as a bed for the skunk. When it was time for dinner, Tipper put the skunk in the box, tied the lid on it, and set it on the back porch. When they finished eating, she went to check on the skunk. She discovered that Mandy had gnawed through the box and escaped.

When Al Gore saw how disappointed she was, he grabbed a flashlight and said, "I think I can find it."[12] Tipper went along to help. They returned about an hour later, with a skunk. Once they were inside the house where it was light, Al Gore was able to get a better look at the animal. He realized that it was the wrong skunk! They raced for the door with the skunk, but the animal got scared and sprayed them before they could get outside.

In spite of that smelly episode, Tipper Aitcheson made a good impression that weekend. Pauline Gore later wrote about Tipper and her first visit to the farm: "Very young, beautiful and cheerful, she brightened life in the entire household."[13]

Tipper graduated from high school in 1966.

Tipper graduated from Garland College with a degree in early-childhood education. She then transferred to Boston University, where she majored in psychology, the study of the mind and of human behavior. She says her decision to study psychology probably had something to do with her parents' divorce. Her own experience made her more aware of other people's feelings.

Like many other college students at the time, she marched in support of civil rights and protested the war in Vietnam. She enjoyed being an activist. "There was a feeling that you were making a commitment with other people for something that was much greater than all of you for an ideal," she later said.[14] The Vietnam War would soon have an even bigger impact on her life.

Love and War

Al Gore proposed to Tipper when she was a junior in college and he was a senior. The one thing that threatened to spoil their happy time was the Vietnam War. "You didn't think about getting on with your life, you thought about getting through the war, stopping the war," Tipper Gore has said.[1]

At that time, all young men age eighteen and older had to register for the military draft. Those who were in college could delay being drafted until they finished their schooling. Now Al Gore was graduating. It was very possible that he would be drafted immediately after college and sent to Vietnam to fight in a war he did not believe in.

Vietnam is a small country in Southeast Asia that

had been a French colony and was later divided into two parts. Communists controlled North Vietnam. In South Vietnam, the government was anti-Communist. Fighting began when Communists from North Vietnam invaded South Vietnam.

The first United States troops were sent to help the South Vietnamese in the early 1960s. At that time, most Americans supported the war because they believed it was very important to stop the spread of communism. Communist countries are ruled by dictators, and the government owns everything. America is a democracy, a system in which people elect their rulers and citizens can own property. In the 1960s, the American government warned that if one country fell to communism, others would follow. This was called the "domino theory."

Americans thought that with their larger, better-equipped forces they would quickly defeat the North Vietnamese Army. But fighting the North Vietnamese and the Viet Cong—as Communist rebels in South Vietnam were called—was harder than anyone expected. Much of the fighting took place in the jungles. That gave an advantage to the Vietnamese troops. While it was unfamiliar territory to Americans, it was home to the Vietnamese. Many American soldiers were injured or killed by booby traps that the North Vietnamese set up in the jungles.

It was soon clear that the war would not end as soon as Americans had hoped. More and more young men were drafted and sent to fight in a war that appeared to have no end in sight. By 1967, more than half a million American soldiers were fighting in

Vietnam, and Americans were discouraged about the war.

Some of the most vocal critics against the war were college students. Many were angry that America was interfering in a civil war on the other side of the world when there were plenty of problems here in the United States. They also thought that the United States was more involved in the war than the South Vietnamese themselves were. The students held demonstrations on campuses all across the United States. Some of the demonstrations turned violent when students clashed with police who were trying to keep order.

In 1968, Richard Nixon was elected president of the United States. His policy of "Vietnamization" called for a gradual replacement of American troops with South Vietnamese soldiers. That plan would not go into effect immediately, and it was too late for Al Gore, who graduated that spring. He knew he would very likely be drafted and possibly sent to Vietnam.

Some young American men moved to Canada to avoid the draft. According to some reports, Al Gore thought about this. Those same reports said his mother would support that decision if that was what he decided to do. Tipper Gore later said that he never seriously considered that choice. She and Al Gore were making wedding plans, and living in Canada was not something they had discussed.[2]

Al Gore decided not to wait to be drafted. Instead, he enlisted in the Army. Some say he did it to help his father, Al Gore, Sr., who was preparing for his 1970 reelection race for the Senate. His opponent was

William Brock, heir to the Brock Candy Company. Already it was shaping up to be a heated campaign that centered on one key issue—the fact that Al Gore, Sr., opposed the war in Vietnam.

Al Gore, Jr., said he enlisted for another reason. His draft board was in the small town of Carthage, Tennessee. A set number (a quota) of young men from that community would be expected to serve their country. He believed that if he refused to fight, one of his friends would be drafted instead. He did not want to think that his friend would be sent off to war in his place. "I couldn't see myself attending his going-away party, then walking down Main Street as if nothing had happened," Al Gore once said.[3]

When Gore graduated from Harvard, the Army sent him to Fort Dix in New Jersey. After basic training, he was stationed at Fort Rucker in Alabama, where he worked on the base newspaper.

Tipper continued her studies at Boston University, where she still had a year left to complete her bachelor's degree. By that time, Nixon's "Vietnamization" plan was in effect. In the spring of 1970, as American troops began to pull out of Vietnam, the North Vietnamese invaded Cambodia, a neighboring country. President Nixon responded by sending American troops and bombs to Cambodia.

This made many Americans angry. Just when they thought the war in Vietnam was about to end, American soldiers were being sent to fight in another Asian country. Students protested on campuses all across the United States. The demonstrations quickly turned violent. On May 4, four students at Kent

State University in Ohio were shot and killed by Ohio National Guardsmen assigned to crowd control. The killing of unarmed students made others even angrier and set off more protests and strikes at universities across the country.

At Boston University, which Tipper attended, students reacted with the worst violence in the school's history. It began in the administrative buildings, where fire bombs exploded on May 5. Then fires were set in the university's School of Fine Arts.

Fearing that there would be more violence, many universities closed down and sent the students home early. Administrators at Boston University decided to do the same. They also canceled graduation ceremonies that spring. Tipper earned her bachelor's degree in psychology in May 1970. Like the other students in her class, she received her diploma by mail.

That same month, on May 19, Tipper married Private Al Gore, Jr. Her mother and both of her grandmothers helped her pick out her wedding gown. According to tradition, it is bad luck for the groom to see the bride in her wedding dress before the ceremony. Tipper followed tradition, and Al Gore did not see her in her gown until she walked down the aisle at their wedding.

The wedding took place in the Washington Cathedral in Washington, D.C. Tipper was twenty-one, and Al Gore, Jr., was twenty-two. They had to get special permission from the minister to have the Beatles song "All You Need Is Love" played during the ceremony.

After the ceremony, a reception was held at a

country club in Alexandria, Virginia. The newlyweds and their guests danced to popular tunes of the 1960s. "I was so happy, I could have danced all night," Tipper Gore recalled.[4]

The Gores honeymooned in Hawaii and then moved into their first home—a trailer park in Daleville, Alabama. It was near the base where Gore was stationed. "It was great," Tipper Gore said. "We were newly married, we were in love, it was fabulous."[5]

The Gore family was very active in Senator Albert Gore's reelection campaign. Nancy Gore was her father's campaign manager. Al Gore, Jr., helped whenever he got time off on the weekends. Tipper Gore also made appearances for her father-in-law's campaign.

In spite of their efforts, Senator Gore lost his reelection bid. He had spent thirty-two years in Congress—fourteen years in the House and eighteen years in the Senate. His loss was a big disappointment for the whole family. "When he lost, it was the same feeling you have when somebody dies," Tipper Gore recalled.[6]

The following month, on Christmas Day, Al Gore, Jr., left for an assignment in Vietnam. "It was a rough time," Tipper Gore remembered. "The war was raging. Al's father had just been defeated in a very nasty election (largely because of his opposition to the war), Nixon was president; it was all very depressing."[7]

Al Gore became a reporter with the Army's 20th Engineering Brigade. His job was to write about the war for Army newspapers. He sent some of the articles he wrote to his wife. She sent them to the editor

Newlyweds Tipper and Al Gore, Jr., chat with his parents, Pauline and Senator Al Gore.

of a Nashville newspaper, the *Tennessean*. The editor published them in the newspaper.

Al Gore served six months in Vietnam. In May 1971, he returned to the United States and received his honorable discharge from the Army. Al and Tipper Gore moved to Carthage, Tennessee, and settled on a farm across the river from Al Gore's parents.

Tipper Gore plunged into the life of a farmer's wife with the same kind of enthusiasm that she had for almost everything she did. She planted a vegetable garden, refinished furniture, and sewed drapes for the house.

Her husband, on the other hand, had trouble deciding what he wanted to do. "He was more restless," Tipper Gore has said, recalling how he had changed.[8] She would wake up during the night and find he was gone. He would be out walking around the farm, unable to sleep.

It was a common problem for Vietnam veterans. In other wars, the soldiers were welcomed home as heroes. That was not always the case for soldiers returning from Vietnam. Some Americans who opposed the war criticized those who fought in it. This confused returning soldiers who believed they had fought for their country.

Al Gore started a small home-building business but decided it was not what he wanted. That fall he enrolled at Vanderbilt University's divinity school. Although divinity school is usually for people studying to become ministers, that was never what Al Gore planned to do. He said that after his experience in Vietnam, he wanted time to study and think about spiritual things. He also got a job as a reporter for the *Tennessean*. He worked the night shift at the newspaper and attended school during the day.

Nashville was about an hour's drive from Carthage. Because of his busy schedule, Al Gore was not able to make the drive every day. Tipper Gore was commuting to Nashville, too. At her husband's urging, she signed up for a photography course. Her instructor was the photo editor at the *Tennessean*, and the classes were held in Nashville.

The Gores decided that it would be easier for them to move to Nashville instead of driving back and forth so often. They rented a duplex apartment in Nashville for a while and later bought a home there.

On August 6, 1973, their daughter Karenna was born. Tipper Gore said their daughter's name was inspired by the pretty name Anna Karenina, the main character in a novel by Russian writer Leo Tolstoy. Tipper Gore was reading *Anna Karenina* while she was pregnant.

Gore did so well in her photography class that she was offered a part-time job at the *Tennessean*. She also decided to work toward her master's degree in psychology and enrolled at George Peabody College (now part of Vanderbilt University).

Tipper Gore discovered that photography could be a powerful tool in working for social change. For example, she took a photograph of a woman who had been evicted from her home. After the photograph was published in the *Tennessean*, people contacted the paper offering to help the woman.

Al Gore also discovered the power of the press

when he began working as a police reporter for the newspaper. Through careful research, he was able to uncover corruption in the Nashville city council. He was then assigned to report on the trials of the council-men who were charged as a result of his findings. While Gore was covering the trials, he became inter-ested in the law and how the court system worked. In 1974, he left divinity school and enrolled in Vanderbilt's law school.

Tipper Gore earned her master's degree in psychology from George Peabody College in 1975. She was still working part-time at the *Tennessean* and was thinking about beginning studies for her Ph.D. degree. She thought she might become a child psychologist. "I never felt tremendous pressure to have a career," she said, "but I wanted to do something meaningful. I wanted to be helpful."[9] Her plans soon changed.

Early in 1976, Al Gore learned that the congress-man from the Fourth Congressional District in Tennessee was retiring after thirty years in the House of Representatives. It was the same seat that Gore's father once held. Because he still owned a farm in that district, Al Gore was eligible to run for the House seat.

Making a Difference

Al Gore later said that even he was surprised at how quickly he decided to get into the race for the House. On the other hand, it seemed like a natural choice. Because of his father's years in Washington, politics had played a large part in Al Gore's early years. Perhaps the role of politician had always been in the back of his mind. It was simply a matter of waiting for the right time.

"It just came home to me that if I was ever going to do it, now was the time," Al Gore said. "Not ten years from now. Not one week from now. Now."[1]

Unfortunately, Tipper Gore had no chance to prepare for this change in plans. "That was a bombshell," she said later, recalling his decision. "He was thinking about being a writer and combining it with law. We were going in a very different direction. So it was a shock."[2] Suddenly, she had a new role. As the wife of a politician, she would be expected to campaign for her husband.

Tipper Gore was not sure she wanted to spend all her time campaigning. She enjoyed her work as a part-time photographer at the *Tennessean*, and she was not ready to give it up. At first, she planned to continue working at the newspaper and to campaign on her days off.

It was her boss at the newspaper who convinced her to take time off to work full-time on the campaign. He said that if Al Gore did not win the election, she could come back to the newspaper. Her job would be waiting for her.

The Gores put their house in Nashville up for sale. Then they moved back to their farm in Carthage and began planning their campaign strategy.

Al Gore held a press conference in front of the court-house in Carthage to announce that he was going to run. He was so nervous about giving his first speech that he threw up in the men's room at the courthouse before going out to make his announcement.

Campaigning was not easy for Tipper Gore, either. "I was very hesitant," she recalled. "I could hardly bring myself to go up to someone and say, 'Do you think you could vote for my husband?'"[3]

Al Gore would not let his father campaign for him. He wanted to win on his own, without the benefit of his father's influence. He did get expert advice from his sister, Nancy, who had been involved with all of their father's campaigns.

Tipper Gore says that as they gained experience in campaigning, they began to enjoy it. They felt closer as a couple because they were working together for a common goal—Al Gore's election to Congress.[4]

Gore won that election, and the family moved to Washington, D.C., in January 1977. They settled into the home Tipper Gore had grown up in, which they bought from her grandmother. At that time Tipper Gore was expecting their second child, daughter Kristin, who was born on June 5, 1977.

Al Gore soon earned a reputation as a hardworking

Tipper and little Karenna Gore join Al Gore, Jr., during his 1976 campaign for Congress. Tipper Gore has said that campaigning was hard for her at first, but after a while she began to enjoy it.

congressman. Many nights he worked late on Capitol Hill. He was also determined not to lose touch with the people he represented in the House. To prevent that, he went back to Tennessee almost every weekend. On Friday nights he flew to Tennessee, where he held town meetings on Saturdays. Sunday mornings he flew back to Washington, D.C., arriving in time to attend church services with his family. Sunday afternoons were reserved for family activities. "Friday he was gone, Sunday he was back," Tipper Gore recalled.[5]

Once again Tipper Gore had to make adjustments in her life. "Campaigns are for the two of you, an equal partnership, but then you wake up and he's been elected to office," she said. "It's a rude awakening."[6] Al Gore was busy with matters of Congress, and she had to make a life for herself.

She began by forming a group called the Congressional Wives Task Force. Members met weekly to discuss subjects such as domestic violence, nutrition, and problems of the elderly. They brought in experts to speak to the group about these topics.

Another concern of the task force was the amount of violence being shown on television. Gore joined with the national Parent-Teachers Association (PTA) and several other groups to express her concern about the violence and how it was affecting young people. Gore served as chairperson of the Congressional Wives Task Force in 1978.

Members of the House of Representatives are elected for two-year terms. In 1987, Al Gore was unopposed in his reelection bid for another term in the House. He began his second term in January

1979. That same month, the Gores' third daughter, Sarah, was born.

Tipper Gore served as chairperson of the Congressional Wives Task Force again in 1979. She was also busy maintaining two homes—their home in Arlington and their farm in Carthage, where the family spent Christmases and summers. Still, she wanted to do more.

Having her husband gone on the weekends meant that she did not have much of a social life. Most of the social events in Washington take place on weekends, and she did not feel comfortable attending them by herself. She spent a lot of time at home alone with three young daughters. "One of the ways I helped fill the void was by building a darkroom, which I did shortly after Sarah was born," she later wrote.[7]

Soon she was working as a freelance photographer. One of her photographs was published in the *Washington Star,* and others appeared in the *Washington Post.* Most of her work was done for trade journals. These are magazines published for people in a specific business or organization. Trade journals are often smaller than other magazines, and deadlines for these publications are not usually as rushed as those for newspapers. "I found that it was better to work with those types of publications because I could set my own schedule. I had young children," Gore explained.[8]

In 1980, Al Gore was reelected to a third term in the House. Tipper Gore campaigned for her husband in each election and was gaining experience in speaking to large groups. Al Gore was running for his fourth term when their son, Albert Gore III, was born on

The Gore family in Nashville in 1979.

October 19, 1982. The following month, Al Gore, Jr., won his reelection campaign.

Because her husband was often gone, Tipper Gore had much of the responsibility for the day-to-day activities of raising their children. With four children, she had less time to spend on photography, and she eventually gave up her freelance work.

Tipper Gore has said that she never regretted giving up her career for her husband's: "If I'd wanted to go for my own career and get somebody to take care of the children, I would have done that. I truly did not wish to."[9]

In 1984, after eight years in the House, Al Gore ran for a Senate seat from Tennessee. Once again Tipper Gore was busy campaigning. One sad note during Gore's campaign was when his sister, Nancy, the only one in the family who smoked, was diagnosed with lung cancer. She did not live to see Al Gore elected to the Senate on November 6. He received 61 percent of the votes—more votes than any other candidate in Tennessee's history.

In the meantime, Tipper Gore decided to get involved with a problem in their community. She and her children were on their way home after having lunch with Al Gore on Capitol Hill one day. As they waited for a stoplight, the children noticed a shabbily dressed woman on the corner. The woman was gesturing and talking as if she were having a conversation with another person. But there was no one around.

"Who is she talking to?" one of the Gore children asked.[10]

Tipper Gore explained that the woman was probably mentally ill and was seeing someone or hearing voices. She also said that the woman was homeless.

It was the children's first up-close encounter with a homeless person, and they were shocked. They wanted to take her home, but Tipper Gore said that was not a good idea. Instead, they went home and talked about what they could do. The plan they came up with was to volunteer at shelters for the homeless, something the Gore family continues to do.

In December 1984, another concern attracted Gore's attention. She had purchased *Purple Rain*, a popular record album by the artist then known as Prince. It was a gift for her eldest daughter, eleven-year-old Karenna, who had heard the song "Let's Go Crazy" on the radio several times and liked it.

Gore regretted her purchase when she heard the lyrics of another song on the album. She thought they were inappropriate for preteens. About the same time, her two younger daughters were asking questions about music videos that were being shown on television. These music videos showed scantily clad women in cages or handcuffed. In one video, a woman appeared to be dead and was wrapped in barbed wire. Another showed a man using electricity to knock people off a building. These images were frightening for small children. Tipper Gore decided to take action.

"If something affects her kids, she is not just going to sit around and talk about it," a former coworker from the *Tennessean* noted. "She gets involved and makes something happen. She really believes she can make a difference, and she does."[11]

Battling the Record Industry

Gore discovered that her friends were also very concerned about music that was being sold to their children. The songs had explicit references to sex, violence, and the occult or supernatural. Gore said some songs glamorized suicide and encouraged the use of drugs and alcohol. She thought there should be a way to let parents know that an album might contain these types of lyrics.

In February 1985, Gore and her friend Susan Baker formed the Parents Music Resource Center (PMRC). Baker was the wife of Republican James Baker, who was then secretary of state. More friends, including the wives of other congressmen from both parties, joined them.

The PMRC first proposed an album rating system

like the one being used for movies. The group also wanted song lyrics to be printed on the outside cover of an album. "There is no way to judge what our children are being exposed to," Gore said. "If they're going to sell a product like this, then they could at least give us a consumer warning."[1]

Members of the PMRC worked from their kitchen tables, sending letters and getting the word out by participating in radio call-in shows. The group soon got national attention. Newspaper reporters called to ask for interviews. Tipper Gore and Susan Baker were invited to appear on television shows such as *Today*, *Good Morning America*, *The Phil Donahue Show*, and *Entertainment Tonight*.

Many people in the recording industry were against a rating system. One reason was that there were so many albums produced each year. Although the rating system on movies appeared to be working, the number of films released each year was far smaller than the number of albums produced. The motion picture industry rated about 325 films a year. The recording industry, on the other hand, would have to rate about 25,000 songs a year. In response to this concern, the PMRC shifted its proposal to a generic warning or parental advisory. This would take the place of the more time-consuming rating system.

Some people were against even a generic labeling system. Their fear was that warning labels would open the door to censorship. Once the word *censorship* came up, arguments became heated. It was like waving a red flag in front of Americans, who have always treasured their freedom of speech.

Tipper Gore talks with other members of the Parents Music Resource Center, a group concerned about the offensive lyrics of some popular music. From left are Tipper Gore, Susan Baker, Sally Nevis, and Pam Howar.

Censorship means keeping information from people. Tipper Gore said that the PMRC wanted just the opposite. It wanted to get *more* information out to parents about the kind of music that was available to their children. "The material has a right to be there," she said. "But we said that, as parents in the marketplace, we have a right to know beforehand what's there."[2]

Their critics insisted that the PMRC wanted something much different. "They convinced people we wanted to ban music," Gore noted.[3]

Gore had gained valuable experience as a public speaker while campaigning for her husband. She became the spokesperson for the PMRC. As a result, she became the target of personal attacks from people who were against a labeling system for records. "They saw me as a book-burning, prudish housewife who obviously was bored with nothing better to do," she said.[4]

One episode stood out in her mind. She was asked by members of the New York chapter of the National Association of Recording Arts & Sciences (NARAS) to represent the PMRC in a panel discussion. (The NARAS is the group that presents the annual Grammy Music Awards.)

Other members of the panel included a record producer, a jazz artist, and punk rock singer Wendy O. Williams. Gore agreed to be on the panel because she thought it would be an open discussion between people who were for a labeling system and those who were against it. Instead, the discussion seemed more like a personal attack against Gore. "Every question, for almost three hours, was aimed at me," she later wrote. "Many were highly personal and insulting. No doubt about it—I had been set up."[5]

Frank Zappa, the founder of the rock group Mothers of Invention, became one of her most outspoken critics. He said that Gore and the other women in the PMRC were using their husbands' positions to pressure the recording industry to adopt a labeling system. "No person married to or related to a government official should be permitted to waste the nation's time on ill-conceived housewife hobby projects like this," Zappa said.[6]

Tipper Gore conceded that their names got people to pay attention to what they were saying. Being married to congressmen and senators helped the PMRC members do what other groups, including the national PTA, had not been able to do. "The PTA, which has 5.6 million members, tried for a year and a half to get people to pay attention and got nowhere," Gore said.[7]

Although their husbands' names opened doors, their influence went no further. The PMRC had no plan to pass laws that would force record companies to use the labels, although some other groups did. The PMRC wanted a *voluntary* labeling system, Gore noted.

Gore's work with the PMRC affected other members of her family, too. Karenna Gore said that some of the students at her school teased her about her mother's actions. "They think it's dumb," Karenna told a reporter, "but they don't understand. It's too hard to explain it to them, so I just don't say anything."[8]

Reporters also wondered whether Al Gore supported her efforts. They noted that her campaign could hurt her husband's political career. Tipper Gore said that as a parent, her husband supported what she was doing. The fact that he was a senator had nothing to do with the issue. She said that she had been an activist before she was married. She had protested against the Vietnam War and had worked for civil rights. "This was not the wife of a Senator who had suddenly become active," she later noted.[9]

Some people thought that Tipper Gore and the PMRC were making too much of something that was not that important. After all, parents and their children have disagreed over music for generations. These people also wondered how much a song, which was only a few minutes long, could influence a listener.

Supporters of the PMRC said that music had changed with the debut of the Music Television Network (MTV). Songs were now visual images on television screens. That made them more powerful.

A survey done by a New York–based research firm showed that a majority of Americans supported what the PMRC was doing. According to the survey, 75 percent thought there should be some type of rating system for albums. In addition, 80 percent of those surveyed thought that song lyrics should be printed on album covers.[10]

Early in August 1985, the Senate Commerce Committee announced that it would hold a hearing to see what, if anything, could be done about song lyrics. Leaders in the recording industry were angry about the hearing because Al Gore was on the committee. Some people thought that he had asked for the hearing. Actually, the idea had come from John Danforth, a senator from Missouri, who chaired the committee.

Tipper Gore said that at first she and her husband were against the hearing. They thought it might not be a good idea because of Al Gore's position. (Some critics thought the Gores had a conflict of interest.) But she was not the only PMRC member in that situation. A total of five of the senators on the seventeen-member committee were married to PMRC members.

The hearing was held on September 19, 1985. Tipper Gore, Susan Baker, and Jeff Ling represented the PMRC. Ling was a former rock musician who had become a youth minister. Frank Zappa, John Denver, and Dee Snider from the group Twisted Sister testified on behalf of the recording industry.

It was supposed to be an informational meeting. However, people from the recording industry said that it was the first step toward passing a law to force them to use warning labels. According to an article in *Time* magazine, one senator did make it appear that way. He said that "unless the music industry cleans up its act, there might well be legislation."[11]

The meeting got a tremendous amount of attention. No decisions were made that day, but the hearing made people in the recording industry realize that the problem about song lyrics would not just go away. They were going to have to pay attention to what members of the PMRC were saying.

On November 1, 1985, the Recording Industry Association of America (RIAA) and the PMRC reached an agreement. The president of the RIAA announced that record companies had agreed to start putting warning labels on albums that might contain objectionable lyrics. The labels would read: "Explicit Lyrics—Parental Advisory."[12] Record companies that did not want to use the labels could choose to print the lyrics of the songs on the album cover instead.

The RIAA represented 80 percent of the recording companies. The other 20 percent were independent companies. Some of the independents said that they would not use the warning labels, nor would they print song lyrics on album covers. That did not worry members of the PMRC. They had asked for a *voluntary* labeling system and 80 percent of the record companies was an impressive number.

While Gore's involvement with PMRC was well known, little notice was paid to other things she was

Tipper Gore testifies before the Senate Commerce Committee on behalf of the Parents Music Resource Center. The PMRC wanted warning labels to appear on record albums with explicit lyrics.

doing. She was still very concerned about the problem of homelessness. In 1986, she cofounded Families for the Homeless and became chairperson of the group. The purpose of this organization is to make people more aware of the problems and needs of the homeless.

At the same time, Gore did not give up her efforts to educate parents about violent and explicit song lyrics. She wrote a book, *Raising PG Kids in an X-Rated Society*, which was released in 1987. In the book she described her efforts to get record companies to use a labeling system. She also wrote about music videos, teen magazines, and rock concerts, which were also becoming more explicit.

The book contained actual quotes from songs. That, as some people noted, made the book X-rated. Gore admitted that she would not let her own children read it. "It's for parents. It's not for kids," she said.[13] In an interview, Gore talked about what she wanted the book to do: "I'm hoping that people will be motivated to take some action, whatever they feel comfortable with."[14]

The book got poor reviews, but it sold well. Parents seemed to want more information about their children's music. Gore boosted sales by going on the road to promote her book. In only a few months, more than fifty thousand copies were sold. Gore thought it could have done even better if she had continued to promote it. However, she cut her book tour short to campaign for her husband. He was seeking the Democratic nomination for president of the United States.

A Hard Campaign

Although Al Gore was the one campaigning for office, his wife was better known. People were talking about her work with the PMRC and her book, *Raising PG Kids in an X-Rated Society*. Some of Al Gore's advisors were worried that his wife's book might hurt his campaign.

Gore says her husband never asked her not to talk about her book so that he could win the election. "I think that speaks to our relationship and his courage as a politician," she noted.[1]

The Gores did decide early in the campaign that it would be a good idea for them to meet with leaders from the recording industry to clear the air. That meeting was held in Los Angeles on October 28, 1987. The Gores said it was not a political meeting and that

Tipper and Senator Al Gore, Jr., enjoy a happy moment during Al Gore's run for the Democratic presidential nomination in 1988.

they were not seeking money for Al Gore's campaign. It was meant to be a chance for Tipper Gore to explain her stand on song lyrics. They wanted to make it clear that she was not in favor of censorship, as some of the media had reported. "I stated my position and I stated my opposition to censorship. That was the primary reason that I went," Tipper Gore explained.[2]

The meeting was supposed to be off the record, so members of the press were not allowed to attend. But someone secretly recorded the meeting. A copy of the tape was released to *Variety*, a well-known newspaper in the entertainment business.

The following day, *Variety* published quotes taken from the tape. According to the article, Gore admitted that the Senate Commerce Committee hearing held on September 19, 1985, had been a mistake.

Tipper Gore said the report was not true. The quotes in the article had been heavily edited. "What I said was, I could see how the Senate hearing could be *perceived* by some as political pressure, and that that was a mistake," she later explained.[3]

Gore limited her campaigning to two or three days a week, but not because she thought she would hurt the campaign. She was more concerned about spending time with their four children, who then ranged in age from five to fourteen.

She hoped that people would be able to separate her book from her husband's campaign. "In the book I am speaking for myself, and in his Presidential race my husband will speak for himself," she said. "We're a two-career family."[4]

Gore did not get her wish. Her book was very

much a part of the campaign, and some people showed their support for her. Many times during the campaign, people handed Al Gore copies of his wife's book and asked him to sign it.

Other people were angry with her. They used her campaign appearances to let her know how they felt. For example, she was scheduled to give a speech at the Beverly Wilshire Hotel in Los Angeles, and people began protesting her appearance weeks before she arrived. They borrowed a phrase from a well-known antidrug campaign to use in flyers that they handed out at music stores. The flyers read: "JUST SAY NO TO TIPPER GORE."[5]

Gore heard about the protests, but she did not change her plans to appear. If anything, she became even more determined. "I am not going to be intimidated and threatened by some vigilante groups," she told a reporter, "groups who are out to politicize this issue and hurt my husband."[6]

Workers for Al Gore's campaign were also kept busy defending rumors that kept popping up because of his wife. For example, an article published in the *Washington Post* said that George Mason University in Fairfax, Virginia, had canceled a Frank Zappa concert because of pressure from Tipper Gore and the PMRC. That report was not true. The *Washington Post* printed a correction to the story, but the damage had already been done. Once again the press had suggested that Tipper Gore hated rock music.

On the other hand, she could not be blamed for all of her husband's campaign problems. Al Gore did a good job of campaigning in the South, where he appeared relaxed. In other parts of the country, he came across as too intellectual, stiff, and humorless.

There were several candidates seeking the Democratic nomination. They competed for votes in state primary elections. Gore won primaries in seven states, but it was not enough to get him nominated to run for president. In April 1988, he announced that he was withdrawing from the race. Governor Michael Dukakis from Massachusetts won the Democratic presidential nomination that year. Dukakis lost to Republican George Bush in the general election.

The campaign had a lasting effect on Tipper Gore. She had faced many personal attacks because of her views on objectionable song lyrics. Friends said that the campaign made her less trusting.[7] Before the campaign she was willing to give interviews; after the campaign she was less willing. But she did continue to work for causes that she believed in.

One of her projects was putting together a photo exhibit titled "Homeless in America: A Photographic Project." Gore worked with the National Mental Health Association (NMHA) on this project. The purpose of the exhibit was to raise public awareness of the problems of the homeless.

The exhibit opened at the Corcoran Gallery of Art in Washington, D.C., and then toured cities throughout the United States for two years. Gore traveled to many of those cities, urging people to get involved in finding solutions to homelessness.

Gore was busy with her volunteer work, but she would soon need to cut back. Her family was always her first priority, and in 1989 she had little time for

Al Gore, Jr., with his wife and son at his side, announces his withdrawal from the race for the 1988 presidential nomination.

anything else. That year, on April 3, Al and Tipper Gore and their six-year-old son, Albert, attended a Baltimore Orioles game with friends and neighbors. It was opening day of the baseball season, and they had all enjoyed the outing. They were a happy group as they left the stadium talking about the game.

Al Gore was holding his son's hand. Then, in a split second, Albert squirmed away from his dad, darted into the street, and was hit by a passing car. The impact threw Albert thirty feet through the air. He slid another twenty feet across the rough pavement.

The Gores rushed to their son, who lay next to a curb. He was not moving, and they were not sure if he was even alive. Al Gore immediately began cardiopulmonary resuscitation (CPR) to revive his son.

Two off-duty nurses were among the crowd that gathered at the scene, and they also helped. An ambulance arrived within minutes, but it took a long time for the ambulance crew to get Albert stabilized so that he would survive the trip to the hospital.

". . . Everything Else Stopped"

Albert Gore was taken to Johns Hopkins Children's Center in Baltimore, where he was listed in "serious but stable condition."[1] He had a long list of injuries, including second-degree burns on his body caused by sliding across the pavement. A leg, a few ribs, and his collarbone were broken. He could not use one of his arms because the nerves in it had been badly damaged. He also had a concussion and internal injuries, which included a ruptured spleen and kidney and a bruised lung.

Gore canceled all her appointments so that she could be with her son at the hospital. "The accident happened, and everything else stopped," she recalled.[2] She and her husband got a room in a nearby hotel. They took turns staying with Albert all day and all night at the hospital.

For the first few days, Albert was hooked up to a respirator. This machine helps patients breathe when they are not able to do so on their own.

Albert had several surgeries. One was to remove more than half of his badly damaged spleen. One function of the spleen is to get rid of worn-out red blood cells. The spleen also helps the body fight infections. It is possible to live without this organ, but doctors wanted to save as much of his spleen as they could. Albert also had surgery on his leg. A pin was placed in his left thigh to hold the bone together while it healed.

Although he was in a lot of pain, Albert did not lose his sense of humor. He often joked with nurses and family members while he was in the hospital.

On April 25, he had surgery again. This time doctors removed the pin in his leg. Then he was placed in a body cast that went from his chest to his toes. The next day he went home from the hospital.

The Gores made a public statement thanking all the people who had written. They received more than four thousand letters from well-wishers. Their thoughtfulness meant a great deal to Tipper Gore. "Just a kind word can make a huge difference to a person in pain," she later said. "I try to keep that lesson with me."[3]

Albert was out of the hospital, but there was still a long road to recovery. He depended on his family for his care. With the body cast, he could not even roll over by himself. Someone had to get up several times during the night to help him change his sleeping position. The Gores turned their first-floor dining room

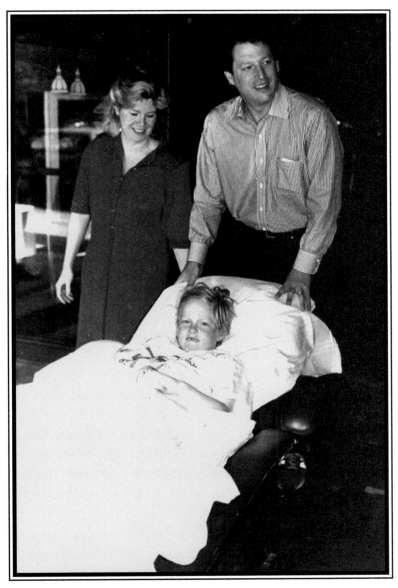

Tipper and Al Gore take their son, Albert, home from the hospital in April 1989. The six-year-old was seriously injured when he darted in front of a car, and it would be a long road to recovery.

into Albert's room. Tipper Gore and her husband took turns sleeping on a mattress on the floor next to his bed. That way they were available when their son needed help during the night.

During this time, the Gores decided to get family counseling. "Our marriage wasn't in trouble," Gore later explained. "Whenever a parent has a child injured, and particularly when you're with the child and you see it happen, you have tremendous guilt."[4]

Tipper Gore noted that some people are embarrassed about getting counseling. She said they should not feel that way. Counseling was a good experience for their family. They learned ways to help Albert during his recovery and also how to help one another.

Gore said that at first she thought she should try to keep their daughters' lives as normal as possible, and not to let their routine be affected by the accident. Counseling helped her understand that the girls needed to help in their brother's recovery. The whole family needed time to heal, and they could do that best by working together.

She gave each of her daughters a job to help Albert. The girls also began taking turns sleeping in the dining room and changing Albert's position during the night. It gave their parents a chance to get some much needed sleep.

Albert spent six weeks in the body cast. After it was removed, he had surgery on his arm to repair nerve damage. Tipper Gore then began helping with his physical therapy. This was a series of daily exercises to strengthen Albert's arm and leg so that he could use them again. It took more than a year, but

Albert made a full recovery. Since then he has been active in sports, including basketball, soccer, baseball, and lacrosse.

Albert's accident made Gore think about how she had been spending her time. She had not realized how busy she was with volunteer work until she began having to cancel appointments to spend time taking care of her son. Volunteering had taken her away from her family. The accident made her more determined to put her family first.

She let their household help go and began doing everything herself. "I drove every carpool and cleaned every john, and I'm glad I did it," she said. "You can learn a lot when you drive a carpool. That's when the kids tell you what's going on."[5]

Gradually, Tipper Gore began volunteering again. Warning labels on record albums were still making news. Many record companies were using the labels, but others were not. Even the companies that were using the labels did not use the same kind. Some lawmakers thought that all the music companies needed to use uniform labels. In at least a dozen states, lawmakers were thinking about passing laws that would force companies to use the labels.

Tipper Gore believed that if the government forced record companies to use the labels, it would be a form of censorship. She spoke out against this legislation. In Louisiana, she testified against a labeling bill that had already been passed. The governor of that state later vetoed the bill.

Leaders of record companies did not want legislators to pass these laws either. They decided that the best way to prevent that from happening was to come up with their own plan for uniform labels that all record companies would use. In March 1990, the companies agreed on a labeling system. The states that were considering laws to force the record companies to use warning labels then dropped their legislative actions.

Leaders in the music industry liked the fact that Tipper Gore had campaigned against laws forcing them to use warning labels. "She stayed faithful to her promise that she was against censorship," one record company executive noted.[6]

Other record company executives had also changed their opinion of Tipper Gore. They now respected her as a woman who could be trusted to keep her word. At that time, Al Gore was running for reelection to the Senate. Some members of the music industry contributed to his campaign.

Gore won reelection to the Senate in 1990. That year, Tipper Gore founded Tennessee Voices for Children. The purpose of this group was to develop programs for children with mental health problems, including emotional and substance abuse. Gore was especially proud of one of the group's achievements— a program called Home Ties. This program promoted home treatment for children with mental health problems. Before then, many of these children were hospitalized for treatment.

Tipper Gore also decided to lose weight. While caring for her son after his accident, Gore had gotten away from exercising and eating healthy foods. As a result, she added twenty-five pounds to her five-foot-five-inch frame. She thought it was time to do something about it.

She did not call her new routine a diet. "I see it not so much as one woman's losing weight as shifting to a lifestyle that is much healthier," she said.[7] With her new way of eating, she also decided to give up diet sodas. She noted that diet sodas have "additives and coloring in them, and you don't need to eat that stuff."[8] Instead, she drank bottled water and fruit juices. She ate low-fat, low-sugar foods, including a lot of fruits, vegetables, and chicken. When she wanted a snack, she reached for pretzels or ginger-snap cookies, which are naturally low in fat.

Another key part of her weight-loss program was exercise. It was Al Gore who encouraged her to begin exercising again. She told him she did not have time. "Make time," he told her.[9] She realized he was right. Being fit would give her the energy she needed to do other things. Gore joined a health club, where she swam and did weight training. She also power-walked. Al Gore gave her a pair of in-line skates as a birthday present, and she began skating with her son. At one point, Tipper Gore was exercising three hours a day.

As she got in better shape, she began jogging. It was not long until she was fit enough to keep up with her husband, and they sometimes jogged together. Other times, she jogged with the family's newest dog, a black Labrador named Shiloh.

The family already had another dog, Coconut, a poodle mix. It was a stray that they had found on their farm in Tennessee one Christmas Eve. They later took in another stray and named it Inspector Turnip.

Exercise keeps Tipper Gore in shape and gives her the energy she needs for her busy life. The in-line skates were a birthday present from her husband.

In 1991, the Gores' eldest daughter, Karenna, graduated from high school. That fall, she began classes at Harvard University, the college her father had attended.

By that time, people were beginning to think about the 1992 presidential election. Many believed that Al Gore would run again. They were surprised when he announced that he would not. Running for president meant at least nine months on the campaign trail. Al and Tipper Gore had talked it over and decided that it would take too much time away from their family.

Although Al Gore had decided not to seek the Democratic nomination for president in 1992, his name came up again as the election got closer. Each political party holds a national convention to select its candidates for president and vice president. The Democratic National Convention would be held in July 1992.

Although the candidates were officially announced at the convention, most of the selection process was done before then. By the end of June, it appeared that the Democratic candidate for president would be Bill Clinton, the governor of Arkansas. The next thing to decide was who would be his running mate. Al Gore was one of the names on Clinton's list.

Al Gore and Bill Clinton had a few meetings to discuss that possibility. A week before the national convention, Clinton's list of choices for a running mate had been narrowed down to what was called the short list, with only a few candidates. Al Gore was one of them.

Although Gore had decided not to run for president, he was interested in being vice president. The

Gores said running for vice president would work out well for them at this time because it would be a short campaign. The election would be held in less than four months. That meant less time away from their children.

The next step was to wait for Clinton's decision. The Gores spent that time at their farm in Carthage. Media people camped out at the end of their driveway, hoping to get a firsthand reaction from the family if Al Gore were selected.

Clinton was expected to make his choice by Wednesday, July 7. By that evening, the Gores still had not been contacted. Then, at 11:00 P.M., the phone rang just as Tipper Gore was getting out of the shower. She picked up the phone and heard Bill Clinton's voice: "Hi, Tipper, I hope I didn't wake you up; and if I did, I needed to."[10]

That night, Clinton asked Al Gore to be his running mate and Gore accepted.

The next day, the Gore family flew to Little Rock, Arkansas. In a ceremony on the lawn of the governor's mansion, Bill Clinton announced his choice of Gore as his running mate. Later that day, the Clintons and Gores traveled to Carthage, Tennessee, Al Gore's hometown, for another round of speeches. Their next stop was New York City, where the Democratic National Convention would begin on Monday, July 13.

The Campaign Trail

The Gores flew into New York City on Sunday, July 12, 1992, the night before the Democratic convention began. They went straight from the airport to a party for the delegates from Tennessee.

Democrats from each state had chosen delegates to represent them at the convention. Each state's population determined the number of delegates the state could send. Altogether, there were five thousand delegates. More than fifteen thousand journalists attended, ready to report on the event.

The Democratic Party had spent $4 million to rent Madison Square Garden for the four-day convention. During that time, the delegates would work on the party platform and officially choose Bill Clinton and

The Clintons and Gores wave from the balcony of the governor's mansion in Little Rock, Arkansas, after Governor Bill Clinton announced that Al Gore, Jr., would be his running mate in the 1992 presidential campaign.

Al Gore as their candidates for president and vice president. The platform is what a political party wants its candidates to talk about during the campaign. It includes the changes they plan to make if they are elected.

Tipper Gore spent that week giving interviews and attending various functions set up by campaign schedulers. Her first appearance at Madison Square Garden was on Thursday evening, the last night of the convention. That was the night Al Gore was selected as the candidate for vice president.

It was an exciting night. Many convention delegates were dressed in red, white, and blue. They cheered often and waved American flags. The room was also decorated in red, white, and blue. A large net hanging from the ceiling held more than sixty thousand balloons to be released during the celebration.

In his acceptance speech, Al Gore talked about his son's accident in 1989. Some people had tears in their eyes as they listened. When he finished, applause and music filled the air.

Tipper Gore smiled broadly as she walked across the stage to give her husband a kiss. She wore a slim-fitting blue dress and her blond hair gleamed under the lights. It was a happy moment, with the crowd cheering and showing its support. The Gores got caught up in the excitement. Suddenly, they began dancing right there on the stage to the music of singer Paul Simon's "Call Me Al." It surprised and delighted people who were not used to seeing Al Gore do something so unexpected.

Some people later criticized Al Gore for talking about his son's accident that night. They said he was using his son to get votes. Tipper Gore did not agree. "He's very much a different person in many ways because of that trauma," she explained, "and if you want to know him, you have to know what happened."[1]

The convention ended on a high note, and the candidates wanted to keep that happy feeling going. The next morning, they began a six-day bus tour that would take them one thousand miles through nine states.

The day started with a rally in Manhattan. People cheered and tossed confetti as the Clintons and

The Gore family during the Democratic National Convention in 1992.

Gores—along with their aides, Secret Service agents, and reporters—climbed into a caravan of eight buses. Two vans followed with television news crews and their camera equipment.

At several planned stops along the way, the candidates visited with people selected in advance. Not planned were the groups of people who gathered along the roadside to greet the candidates. Many times the caravan stopped so the candidates and their wives could get out and shake hands with people along the route.

Because of all these unplanned stops, the tour quickly fell behind schedule. The first overnight was in York, Pennsylvania. The caravan was expected to arrive at 10:00 P.M. but did not get there until almost midnight. Even so, thousands of enthusiastic people were on hand to welcome them.

In the next few months, the Clintons and Gores made seven bus trips, plus two mini-tours lasting less than a day. Everywhere they went, cheering crowds greeted their arrival. This show of support was what impressed Tipper Gore most during the campaign.

Some people made a special effort to see them. Among the crowds, Tipper Gore spotted people in wheelchairs and people with portable oxygen tanks. "One woman said she changed her chemotherapy treatment to see us," Gore recalled in amazement.[2]

The Gores and the Clintons each had their own bus, but about half the time, they chose to ride together. No other candidates and their wives had ever spent this much time with one another and in such close quarters. "It's a major double date," Tipper Gore joked.[3]

Each couple appeared to enjoy the other's company, but some people said that would not last. Campaigning is stressful, and spending so much time together on a bus could strain even a strong friendship. The Gores and Clintons were just getting to know one another.

At first glance, Tipper Gore and Hillary Clinton appeared very much alike. They dressed about the same and both had blond hair, which they wore in about the same style and length. But that was only physical appearances. Their lifestyles were very different.

Hillary Clinton is a lawyer. Earlier in the year, she had made homemakers angry when she tried to explain her choice to have a career. "I suppose I could have stayed home and baked cookies and had teas, but what I decided to do was fulfill my profession," she had said.[4]

Although Tipper Gore had worked as a freelance photographer and had written a book, she considered herself a full-time homemaker and volunteer. She did bake cookies. In fact, one time she baked a batch of sugar cookies while a newspaper reporter interviewed her.

Some people thought it was only a matter of time before two such different women began to disagree. It never happened. "I felt Hillary was my long-lost sister from the moment I met her," Gore said.[5]

Tipper Gore does not like to get involved in discussions about whether it is better to be a stay-at-home mom or to work outside the home. She believes that women need to decide what is right for themselves. While other people saw the differences between Hillary Clinton and Tipper Gore, Gore focused on the ways they were alike.

They were both mothers and both worked for programs to help children. Hillary Clinton had worked for educational reform in Arkansas. She also served on the board of the Children's Defense Fund, a nonprofit organization that helps children in need. The group focuses on prevention—getting programs in place to help children before they drop out of school, get sick, or get in trouble. Special attention is paid to high-risk children, including minorities, the poor, and those with disabilities.

Tipper Gore worked for programs to provide mental health services to children. She was cochair of the Child Mental Health Interest Group. This group, created by the National Mental Health Association, tries to find ways to help children with mental health problems. In 1992, Gore received its first annual Remember the Children Award. The title of that award was later changed to the Tipper Gore Remember the Children Award.

Another thing Hillary Clinton and Tipper Gore had in common was that they were both married to politicians. Because of that, they were able to encourage each other. When one of them was criticized by the press or was tired from a long day of campaigning, the other one understood how she felt.

Curiously, Tipper Gore and Bill Clinton are even more alike: They are both musicians. He plays the

Sharing the excitement at the 1992 Democratic National Convention are Al Gore, Tipper Gore and Hillary Clinton, and Bill and Chelsea Clinton.

saxophone and she plays drums. Both were raised by single mothers, and both are warm, outgoing people married to spouses who do not appear to be at ease with strangers. Tipper Gore said that during the campaign, the four of them often joked about how much she and Bill Clinton had in common.

Before the campaign began, Gore said that she wanted it to be fun. During the next few months she did her best to make it that way. She shook thousands of hands, gave hugs freely, and smiled a lot. She took her camera with her everywhere, ready to capture a special moment on film. Sometimes she even leaned out the window of the moving bus to take a certain photograph. Other times, she stopped the caravan to photograph a child standing on the roadside.

There have been many jokes about politicians kissing babies, but Tipper Gore took that one step further. At a campaign stop in McKeesport, Pennsylvania, she cheerfully planted a kiss on the head of a live llama decorated with campaign signs.

While shaking hands with voters in Minnesota one day, Gore noticed two men in the crowd, each with some kind of animal sitting on his shoulder. As she got closer, she saw that the animals were white rats on leashes. One of the owners held his rat out to Gore. She held the rat and petted it for a moment before moving on to shake hands with other voters.

The candidates and their wives did not do all their campaigning together. There were times when they went in different directions. On September 9, Al Gore was campaigning in New Orleans. That evening he appeared on *Larry King Live*, an interview show on CNN. Tipper Gore had spent the day campaigning in North Carolina. That evening in her hotel room, she flipped on the television to watch her husband. It had been a good day and she was in a playful mood. She felt like doing something mischievous.

Viewers of *Larry King Live* are invited to call in with questions for guests on the show. Gore decided to call. She disguised her voice so that her husband would not recognize it. Then, on live television, she asked him for a date.

Al Gore and Larry King were obviously surprised by this strange caller. Al Gore was also embarrassed, and he had trouble coming up with an answer. He finally managed to say, "I'm not available."[6]

On the other end of the phone line, Tipper Gore laughed and said, "Not even for your wife?"[7]

The next morning, to Tipper Gore's surprise, newspapers all across the country carried stories about her call. It was a glimpse into a marriage that remains strong. Reporters noted that after twenty-two years of marriage, the Gores still appeared to be very much in love. They joked with each other and held hands. At the end of a long day of campaigning, Tipper Gore could be found massaging her husband's tired shoulders.

During the campaign, Tipper Gore occasionally heard boos from the crowds. Some people were still angry with her because of her work with the PMRC. More often, though, people cheered for her.

One California Democrat explained why he thought people had changed their minds about Gore. "Her image changed as people got to know her," he said. "It literally changed from being the weirdo Christian fanatic into somebody who is a great campaigner, a happy woman—and a person with integrity."[8]

Gore was seldom asked about the PMRC during the campaign. She treated it as a thing of the past. In fact, some people were unhappy with her because she did not get involved in a more recent problem over song lyrics. They were upset by the song "Cop Killer" released by the rapper Ice-T and his group Body Count. They said the song promoted violence toward police officers. Tipper Gore did not need to get involved in this controversy because other people were taking charge. When *Raising PG Kids in an X-Rated Society* was released, Gore said she hoped the book would encourage others to take action. Now they were.

Law enforcement groups threatened to lead a boycott against Time Warner, the parent company of the record label marketing the album. A boycott meant that the protesters would not buy any of the company's products. Because of their pressure, the song was removed from the album.

Tipper Gore, in the meantime, was focusing on other issues. During the long bus trips, she talked to Bill Clinton about something she rarely shared with anyone. She told him about her mother's recurring problem with depression, a form of mental illness.

People with depression experience strong feelings of sadness and lose interest in life. When Gore was a child, her mother had these feelings and had to be hospitalized. At that time, in the 1950s, people did not know much about the causes of depression or how to treat it. When people do not understand something, they sometimes fear it. For that reason, Tipper Gore's mother tried to hide her illness.

Even years later, Gore's mother did not talk openly about her illness. "Once when she was in the hospital for something else, I wanted to tell the doctors about the drugs she was on," Tipper Gore later said. "But she didn't want them to know about her condition. It broke my heart."[9]

Tipper Gore wanted to increase awareness of mental health issues. "I want people to understand depression like they understand cancer or heart disease," she explained.[10]

Gore also felt strongly about the issue of family-leave policies. When their son was hospitalized after his accident, Al Gore was able to take time off from work to be with his son. Tipper Gore knew that a leave of absence was not possible for most families. She wanted to change that. "We have a powerful understanding of the fact that other families need to have that opportunity," she said.[11]

Although Gore was busy campaigning, her family was still her first priority. The Gores did not take their children with them when they were campaigning. "We try to keep them insulated from the campaign and out of the press," Al Gore explained.[12]

Tipper Gore arranged her schedule so that she could spend most weekends with her children. On October 19, Albert celebrated his tenth birthday. Gore made sure that no campaign business was scheduled for either her or her husband on that day. The family spent the day together in Washington, D.C.

Another priority for Gore was keeping up the healthy lifestyle that she began when she decided to lose weight. She had not yet reached her goal, and she continued her weight-loss program during the campaign. That was not easy to do. It was hard to find time to eat balanced meals. It was easier to grab whatever was available and eat on the run. There were also dinners that the candidates and their wives were expected to attend. Most of them did not feature low-fat foods.

To help manage her weight, Gore kept fruits and

Tipper Gore and Vice President–elect Al Gore, with singer M. C. Hammer at a dinner during the Inauguration Week activities.

vegetables on hand for snacking. "We became known as the vegetable bus," she later joked. "You'd go to the Clinton bus for doughnuts."[13] At special dinners, she only nibbled on what was served and ate a healthy low-fat meal either before or after the event. She also continued to exercise, usually running about thirty minutes a day.

On November 3, Bill Clinton and Al Gore were elected president and vice president. They received 43 percent of the popular vote. The Republicans—George Bush and Dan Quayle—got 38 percent of the votes, and 19 percent went to Ross Perot, an independent candidate.

Clinton and Gore were sworn into office on

January 20, 1993. That day the sky was clear in Washington, D.C., and the temperature was in the forties. Tipper and Al Gore worked off their nervous tension that morning by jogging to the White House— a seven-mile run.

Just before noon, Tipper Gore stood next to her husband in front of the Capitol. With one hand on a Bible that had once belonged to his sister, Nancy, Al Gore took the oath of office. He was sworn in by retired Supreme Court Justice Thurgood Marshall.

That night the Gores put in appearances at several inaugural balls. During the campaign, Gore had managed to reach her weight goal. She looked slender in a royal blue velvet full-length gown. She also looked happy. Her life as second lady was just beginning.

Second Lady

There were many changes for the family of the new vice president. The biggest difference was getting used to the Secret Service agents who now protected the family twenty-four hours a day.

Tipper Gore said that it was hard for her to adjust to never being alone. It was also difficult for the Gores' teenage daughters and ten-year-old son. The Gore children said it was embarrassing to be picked up after a movie by men in black limousines. The agents in their traditional dark suits stood out in the crowd at school events.

Tipper Gore knew that the Secret Service agents were just doing their job. She also understood that her children did not like feeling different from their friends. She asked the Secret Service agents to use unmarked vans when they took the children somewhere and to dress casually when they attended school functions.

Another change for the family was moving to Admiralty House, the official residence of the vice president. The three-story Victorian-style home is located on the grounds of the United States Naval Observatory. There, powerful telescopes are still used by the Navy to study planets, stars, and meteors.

Admiralty House was built in 1893 and originally served as the home of the superintendent of the Naval Observatory. In 1974, Congress voted to make it the official home of the vice president.

Navy personnel are in charge of the grounds, and Navy cooks prepare meals for the family of the vice president. Gore said having someone else doing the cooking was one of the best parts of being second lady. On the other hand, she did have to train them to fix low-fat meals. "Their idea of vegetables was potato chips," she joked.[1] But she later noted that both the family and visiting dignitaries now complimented the cooks on the meals they prepared.

For a while, the meals were delivered to the Gores at their home in Arlington, Virginia. When Al Gore took office in January 1993, Admiralty House was being repaired. Work included removing asbestos and other harmful materials. New heating and air conditioning were also installed. The Gores did not move in until the work was finished.

In the meantime, Tipper Gore made plans for decorating the house. At her Arlington home, family photos took center stage. The vice president's residence needed to be more formal—at least on the first floor, where official visitors would be entertained. Gore decorated that floor with artwork borrowed from museums.

The one exception to the formality of the first floor was a sparkly red drum set that, for a long time, sat next to a grand piano in the entryway. The drums were a Christmas present from Al Gore to his wife. Tipper Gore had worn out her first set of drums.

Admiralty House would be the Gore family home for the next few years, and they needed to feel comfortable there. For Tipper Gore, that meant neat but casual. Friends say that at home, she is most comfortable in blue jeans.

On the second floor is a family room where the Gores could relax and enjoy time together. Gore had a kitchenette installed next to the family room. That way the children could fix their own snacks instead of going to the kitchen and asking the cooks to prepare something. The home has five bedrooms, enough for each of the four Gore children to have a room. Gore allowed her children to choose the colors for their rooms. The Gores also added a basketball court, which was placed next to the outdoor swimming pool.

Tipper Gore said it was exciting to be moving into such a beautiful home. On the other hand, she also felt sad about leaving her home in Arlington. Except for a few years early in their marriage, it had been her home since she was a small child. The one thing that made Gore feel better was that she was able to rent the house to relatives.[2] At least it was still in the family. She joked about her new role as landlord. "I'm very good at fixing toilets, and I can talk people through fixing the [garbage] disposal," she said.[3]

Gore did not appear upset about moving when the time came. She made the trip to her new home on the back of a Harley-Davidson motorcycle. The bike belonged to Ed Emerson, one of Al Gore's aides. Tipper Gore had called him and asked for a ride.

It was a hot day, and when Emerson and Gore reached Admiralty House, Gore decided to try out the pool. She invited Emerson to join her and lent him one of the extra swimsuits. "For the next twenty minutes the two cannonballed and splashed away the July heat," one reporter wrote.[4]

The Gores settled into Admiralty House, but there were still adjustments to make. Gore says her sixteen-year-old daughter, Kristin, was shocked when she discovered that all her phone calls had to go through the White House operator.[5] Once again Gore tried to make life as normal as possible for her children. She had two private lines installed in the house so that the children and their friends could call one another without using the operator.

The Gore's eldest daughter, Karenna, returned to her studies at Harvard University in the fall of 1993. Kristin and Sarah attended the National Cathedral School, which is only a few blocks from Admiralty House. Albert was a student at St. Albans, the same school his father had attended.

Gore was busy with her duties as second lady. She had her own suite of offices in the Old Executive Office Building, across the street from the White

Tipper and Al Gore enjoy jogging together—for fun, for fitness, and sometimes for charity. In 1993, they led runners in the National Race for the Cure in Washington, D.C.

House. The vice president's office was in the same building. Gore decorated her office with enlarged framed prints of photos she had taken. One photo showed a young Albert Gore III peeking out from under an American flag.

Gore had a six-person staff that was paid for by the Office of the Vice President, but she was a volunteer. She tried to arrange her schedule so that she worked only three days a week, Tuesday through Thursday. That was not always possible.

Although there is no official job description for the wife of the vice president, there are some things she is expected to do. These include traveling with the vice president on some official trips and entertaining visiting dignitaries. Other than that, the job of second lady becomes an individual one. Some vice presidents' wives have stayed in the background, but it is Tipper Gore's nature to be active. She saw her new position as an opportunity to make people aware of various problems.

Her time was also in demand by others. Because of her personality, some people at the White House saw Gore as a good salesperson for the administration. They wanted her to spend a lot of time traveling and talking to people. President Clinton also had an important job for Tipper Gore.

There was growing concern throughout the country about the rising costs of health care. One of Clinton's first acts as president was to set up the Task Force on National Health Care Reform. The group's job was to study the health care problem and find out what could be done about it. Clinton made Gore his Mental Health Policy Advisor.

She traveled throughout the country speaking to groups about mental health. One thing she wanted people to understand is that mental illnesses can be treated. She wanted a policy that would look upon mental health problems in the same way it looks upon physical illnesses. In 1993, she testified before Congress in an effort to get insurance companies to give mental illnesses the same coverage as physical illnesses.

Many people did not agree with her plan. The main reason was that they thought it would cost too much. Gore said that mental illnesses were already expensive. An example she noted was the high cost of hospital care. She said it would be less expensive to treat people with mental illnesses before they needed to be hospitalized.

Once again Gore was trying to get support for something that many people were against, but she did not back down. Her work for better insurance benefits for people with mental illnesses showed one of her best personality traits and, at the same time, one of her worst. Some people admired her ability to work tirelessly for a cause that was important to her. Others saw that as stubbornness. "Tipper embraces a cause so wholeheartedly that she has trouble understanding when people don't see things her way," one reporter wrote.[6]

The President's health care plan was later defeated, but Tipper Gore was successful in making people more aware of mental health issues. "A lot of people view people with mental illness as being weird, different, freaky," one researcher noted. "Coming from her, it becomes something less frightening."[7]

Gore's work helped change the way the government handled mental health questions on government job applications. People applying for jobs no longer had to reveal whether they had received family or marriage counseling.

Tipper Gore also became special advisor to the Interagency Council on the Homeless. At that time there were seventeen agencies with programs for the homeless. Some of them were offering the same programs. One of Gore's jobs was to work with representatives from each of those agencies to coordinate their efforts. They talked about what each agency was doing, what programs were working, and how they could avoid duplicating services.

On Friday mornings, Tipper Gore worked as a volunteer on a Health Care for the Homeless van. She went out on the streets to give medical attention to homeless people and to help them find a place to live. Part of her work was to get homeless people to trust her. "It's a real problem to deal with people who think they don't want to be helped," she said.[8]

Gore noted that her interests in mental health issues and homelessness were closely related. Many people are homeless because they are mentally ill and cannot work. "Although mental illness doesn't explain all homelessness, it does account for about 30 percent of it," she said.[9]

Perhaps because of her background in psychology, Gore is sensitive to what people need and when. In

1993, a terrible flood hit the town of Winfield, Missouri, located north of St. Louis. Gore waited until seven months after the flood to visit. She knew that by that time, the people would just be getting over the shock of the flood. When that happened, they might start feeling depressed about the way it had affected their lives. She thought they might need someone to listen then. She could also give them ideas about where they could get help for this difficult part of their recovery.

Although being second lady gave Gore more visibility for the causes she believed in, her concern for others is also personal. In a 1994 interview, Al Gore gave an example. He said he and his wife had been jogging together when they went by a man huddling on a bench. Al Gore admitted that he hardly noticed the man. "I've seen so many homeless people that I confess to have become a bit numbed," he said. "But when we got home, she put together a container of hot soup and headed right back out."[10]

Tipper Gore's trip to Rwanda in the summer of 1994 was also personal. Civil war in that African country had claimed five hundred thousand lives. Thousands of people, including children, were left homeless. They suffered from malnutrition and diseases such as cholera and dysentery. Gore spent two days helping with relief operations in Rwanda. "Sometimes all a doctor needed was someone to hold an IV bag or help get someone to a field hospital," she explained, "and so I did it."[11] She also fed and bathed orphans.

Gore often traveled to other countries with her husband on official business. She took her camera with her on those trips to places like Russia, Egypt, Haiti, England, and Spain. That gave her another idea—a photo exchange for children.

When Gore visited schools, she talked to the students about photography. She had the students take pictures of themselves and their communities. Then Gore arranged for them to exchange photos with children from another country.

When she was not busy being second lady, Gore could often be seen in-line skating or jogging. There is a quarter-mile track at the vice president's home, but Gore did not like the idea of running in a circle. Her favorite jogging route was the five miles between Admiralty House and Capitol Hill.

She also attended her children's school activities. The Gore children were active in sports, and either Al or Tipper, usually both, attended all their games. Surprisingly, being vice president gave Al Gore more time for family activities. As a congressman, he had to attend many night sessions and spent most weekends in Tennessee holding discussions with the people he represented. As vice president, he had more control over his hours and was home most weekends.

During Al Gore's first term as vice president, Tipper Gore continued to find ways to reach out to others. In 1995, an AIDS clinic in Washington, D.C., honored her with their Friends for Life Award in appreciation for the work that she did for the clinic. She also received the Distinguished Service to Families Award from the American Association of Marriage and Family Therapy.

That year Al and Tipper Gore celebrated their

Tipper Gore likes to share her love of photography with young people. Here, in 1995, she photographs the National Christmas Tree from a hydraulic lift during the ceremony to place a star atop the tree. Looking on are two youngsters selected to take part in the event.

twenty-fifth wedding anniversary. They marked the occasion with a trip to Hawaii, where they had spent their honeymoon.

Also that year, Karenna Gore graduated from Harvard University and Kristin graduated from high school. In the fall, Kristin began classes at Harvard. Tipper Gore was at work on her second book. Bill Clinton and Al Gore were making plans for their reelection campaign.

Picture This

Tipper Gore was proud of the fact that in Washington, D.C., the National Museum of American Art and the Woodrow Wilson House had exhibited the photographs she took during the 1992 presidential campaign. Some of those photographs were now part of her new book, *Picture This: A Visual Diary*. The book was published in 1996.

Gore called the book a visual diary because that was how it began. "We don't have much time to write, so that's how I'm keeping my diary," she told a reporter. "I scribble little anecdotes on the back, put them in chronological order and it becomes a visual diary."[1]

The book has some text pages where Gore wrote openly about her life, her family, and what it was like to be second lady. Most of the book is filled with photographs of her family, world leaders, children she met while traveling in other countries, and homeless people. But it was some of the photos of the vice president that got the most attention.

One photo was of Al Gore taken early in their marriage. Tipper Gore had been studying photography then, and one of her assignments was to take a photograph of someone who loved her. She took one of her husband while he was shaving. In that photo, a bare-chested Al Gore, with part of his face covered with shaving cream, looks into the camera. There are other photos of him taken at the beach and in a hotel swimming pool. In those photos he is dressed in swimwear.

People were surprised that Gore would publish what they said were intimate photographs. Reporters asked Gore whether her husband was embarrassed about the photos and whether this was some new kind of campaign strategy.

"These are pictures that I've had by my bedside table for years, and I've tried to publish them before, and he'd say no. Finally, in this context, he relented," Gore explained.[2]

Perhaps the fact that the book was for a worthy cause was part of the reason he agreed to publishing the photos. All the royalty payments that Tipper Gore earned from the book would be given to organizations helping the homeless and mentally ill.

During the summer of 1996, Gore divided her time between a book tour and campaigning for her husband. At the end of August, Gore was in Chicago promoting her book. She was on the last leg of a book tour that had taken her to twelve cities in nine days.

When she was not signing autographs or talking to reporters, she took time to visit with people who were once homeless and had been helped off the street. One of the people she visited was a man who was living in a room at the YMCA. He had once played flute in the U.S. Army Band. Later, because of problems with mental illness, he ended up homeless.

Tipper Gore visited with him in his room at the YMCA. It was a hot day and he was dressed in a black suit that was obviously too warm. Gore understood that he had taken great care to dress for this meeting and that he was wearing the best clothes he owned. She complimented him on how nice he looked.

Long after she had gone, the man was proudly showing his friends the copy of Gore's book that she had given him. Inside she had written: "Congratulations—on your new life! Love, Tipper."[3]

Gore finished her book tour and then had fourteen hours in Washington before she had to fly back to Chicago for the start of the Democratic National Convention. Reporters soon learned how she managed the stress of such a busy schedule—exercise and humor.

The morning after she arrived in Chicago, reporters waited for her in the basement of her downtown hotel. She soon appeared dressed in a pink jogging suit. She and the reporters set off on a combination interview and early morning run.

Two Secret Service agents also accompanied Tipper Gore. One ran in front of her and one behind.

Gore holds a copy of her second book, Picture This: A Visual Diary, *which showcases her talents as a photographer. Her profits from sales of the book are given to charity.*

As they jogged alongside Lake Michigan, Gore commented on how clean the water looked. She said she might jump in after her run. Reporters thought she was probably kidding.

At the end of the run, Gore took another look at the lake. Then, before anyone knew what was happening, she took off her shoes and jumped into the water. A reporter jumped in with her as if it were part of the interview.

Gore was not content just to wade into the lake. She plunged down into the water, head and all. When she came up again, her hair was plastered tight to her head and water streamed down her face. "Is my mascara running?" she asked.[4] Then she laughed and a camera clicked. The photo appeared in the *Washington Post* the next day.

Bill Clinton and Al Gore were reelected in a campaign that lacked much of the excitement of the 1992 campaign. Once again Tipper Gore stood next to her husband on a cold January morning as he was sworn in as vice president.

During Al Gore's first four years as vice president, most of the newspaper stories and magazine articles written about the Gores were positive. That began to change shortly after the beginning of Al Gore's second term. People began raising questions about Democratic fund-raising activities that had taken place before the election. By March, Tipper Gore was also included in the controversy.

The Federal Election Commission was concerned about five "coffees," meetings that she hosted in the vice president's residence in 1995 and 1996. The people who attended the coffees included community and business leaders who later contributed to the Democratic campaign fund.

It is illegal to conduct fund-raising events in homes or offices owned by the government. The question was, did Tipper Gore ask for campaign donations at those coffees? Those who attended the coffees said no. Tipper Gore was traveling with the vice president in China at the time that the question came up, and she could not be reached for comment.

Once again Tipper Gore was reminded of how quickly life can change for a person who lives in the public eye. Whatever would happen, she appeared to be content to wait it out. She had happier things to think about. Karenna Gore had announced her engagement and the mother of the bride had a wedding to help plan.

On July 12, 1997, twenty-three-year-old Karenna Gore married Andrew Newman Schiff, a thirty-one-year-old doctor from New York City. Aretha Franklin sang for about three hundred guests who attended the wedding in Washington National Cathedral. It was the same cathedral where Al and Tipper Gore had exchanged vows twenty-seven years earlier. After the ceremony, a reception was held at Admiralty House.

Schiff had run for a New York City council seat in 1996. Reporters suggested that the Gores might have another politician in the family. If Karenna Gore had asked her mother for advice about a life in politics, Gore might have advised her not to take it too seriously. "This town [Washington, D.C.] is *very* serious, a little too serious," Gore once said. "To enjoy life

During the 1996 Democratic National Convention in Chicago, Tipper Gore and three of her children meet Chicago White Sox player Lyle Mouton. With Tipper Gore, from left to right, are Sarah, 17; Albert, 15; and Kristin Gore, 19.

you've got to have work that's extremely rewarding, but you've also got to have a sense of play and time to yourself."[5]

Tipper Gore has been successful in all three of those areas. Her family has always been her first priority, but she has also found time to work for causes that she believes are important. She has made time for herself to grow as a photographer, and she always appears to be enjoying it all.

During Al Gore's second term as vice president, Tipper Gore has continued to be an active second lady. In 1997, she celebrated the Mental Health Parity Act. The word *parity* means equal. Passage of this bill was a partial victory for Gore in her work to get insurance companies to cover mental health illnesses just as they cover physical illnesses. It still did not make mental health coverage equal to coverage for other medical conditions, but it was a first step.

In 1998, Tipper Gore became chair of the National Youth Fitness Campaign of the President's Council on Physical Fitness and Sports. In that position, she encourages young people, especially girls, to get involved in sports. Gore notes that physical fitness is closely related to emotional well-being.

Gore also had the honor of heading the United States Presidential Delegation to the 1998 Winter Olympic Games in Nagano, Japan. She wrote daily columns about the Olympics and sent back digital photographs, which appeared on her Internet Website. Gore says the Internet is something that she is learning more about every day. Because of that interest, she began writing a monthly on-line column called "In Focus."

Vice President Gore has had a longtime interest in preserving the environment. That interest prompted Tipper Gore to begin a preservation effort on the grounds of the Naval Observatory. This landscaping project would restore the property to what it might have looked like at the time the house was built. The project was paid for by donations to the Vice President's Residence Foundation.

Gore also worked with the Department of Housing and Urban Development on a ten-year retrospective of her "Homeless in America" photo exhibit. It was a look back through her photographs of ten years of working to help the homeless.

Gore is an example of how women who chose to put their families first can still have meaningful careers. On the other hand, she does not say that the choices she has made are right for everyone. She encourages young people to do what is right for them and not to be afraid to dream.

A little girl from Russia once asked Gore, "How can I grow to be a Second Lady like you?"[6]

Tipper Gore said, "First, get the very best education that you can. And then maybe you can run for president."[7]

Chronology

1948— Born in Washington, D.C., on August 19.

1966— Graduates from St. Agnes Episcopal School.

1970— Earns a bachelor's degree in psychology from Boston University; marries Al Gore, Jr., on May 19.

1973— Daughter Karenna is born August 6.

1975— Earns a master's degree in psychology from George Peabody College (now part of Vanderbilt University).

1977— Daughter Kristin is born June 5.

1978— Chairs the Congressional Wives Task Force.
–1979

1979— Daughter Sarah is born January 7.

1982— Son, Albert III, is born October 19.

1985— Cofounder of the Parents Music Resource Center (PMRC).

1986— Cofounder and chair of Families for the Homeless.

1987— First book, *Raising PG Kids in an X-Rated Society*, is published.

1988— Works with the National Mental Health Association on a photographic exhibit, "Homeless in America: A Photographic Project."

1990— Campaigns against proposed state legislation forcing record companies to use warning labels; founds Tennessee Voices for Children.

1993— Appointed to serve as Mental Health Policy Advisor to the president.

1995— Awarded the Friends for Life Award and the Distinguished Service to Families Award.

1996— Second book, *Picture This: A Visual Diary*, is published.

1998— Becomes chair of the National Youth Fitness Campaign of the President's Council on Physical Fitness and Sports; heads the United States Presidential Delegation to the XVIII Winter Olympic Games in Nagano, Japan; works on a ten-year retrospective of her "Homeless in America" photo exhibit.

Chapter 1. "An American Reunion"

1. Note to the author from Tipper Gore, March 13, 1998.

2. Lois Romano, "Tipper Gore, Playing Down the Rock War: The Candidate's Wife, Defying Protests and Defending Her Man," *Washington Post*, March 29, 1988, p. D8.

3. Tipper Gore, *Picture This: A Visual Diary* (New York: Broadway Books, 1996), p. 20.

Chapter 2. Sports, Pranks, and Teenage Rebellion

1. Colin Greer, "I Know There Is Help," *Parade Magazine*, September 11, 1994, p. 7.

2. Barbara B. Buchholz, "Finding a Niche: Tipper Gore Defines Her Own Role and Style," *Chicago Tribune*, August 21, 1994, sec. 6, p. 5.

3. Barbara Matusow, "Tipper's Revenge," *Washingtonian*, October 1994, p. 139.

4. Stephanie Mansfield, "The Hipper Tipper," *Lear's*, April 1994, p. 82.

5. Ibid., p. 83.

6. Steve Simels, "Tipper's Little Secret," *Entertainment Weekly*, July 24, 1992, p. 8.

7. Jennet Conant, "Family First," *Redbook*, March 1994, p. 82.

8. Jacqueline Trescott, "The Women With a Ticket to Ride: Tipper Gore, Putting the Family First," *Washington Post*, July 16, 1992, p. C2.

9. Sandra McElwaine, "Her Life, Her Love Story," *Good Housekeeping*, March 1993, p. 234.

10. Gail Sheehy, *Character: America's Search for Leadership* (New York: William Morrow and Company, Inc., 1988), p. 195.

11. Note to the author from Tipper Gore, March 13, 1998.

12. Hank Hillin, *Al Gore Jr.: His Life and Career* (New York: Carol Publishing Group, 1992), p. 66.

13. Ibid.

14. Linda Tischler, "Tipper Gore Can't Be Labeled," *Boston Herald*, August 13, 1992.

Chapter 3. Love and War

1. Gail Sheehy, *Character: America's Search for Leadership* (New York: William Morrow and Company, Inc., 1988), p. 203.

2. Lois Romano, "Tipper Gore, Playing Down the Rock War: The Candidate's Wife, Defying Protests and Defending Her Man," *Washington Post*, March 29, 1988, p. D8.

3. Sherrye Henry, "Talking to . . . Albert Gore, Jr.," *Vogue*, May 1988, p. 52.

4. "Tipper Gore Wedding to Albert Gore, Jr.," *People*, February 16, 1998, p. 70.

5. Sandra McElwaine, "Her Life, Her Love Story," *Good Housekeeping*, March 1993, p. 235.

6. Sheehy, p. 205.

7. McElwaine, p. 235.

8. Alex S. Jones, "Al Gore's Double Life," *New York Times Magazine*, October 25, 1993, p. 79.

9. Jennet Conant, "Family First," *Redbook*, March 1994, p. 82.

Chapter 4. Making a Difference

1. Alex S. Jones, "Al Gore's Double Life," *New York Times Magazine*, October 25, 1993, p. 79.

2. Beth Austin, "Tipper Gore: I Am Angry That Children Are Being Exploited," *Chicago Tribune*, April 26, 1987, sec. 6, p. 3.

3. Barbara Matusow, "Tipper's Revenge," *Washingtonian*, October 1994, p. 81.

4. Barbara B. Buchholz, "Finding a Niche: Tipper Gore Defines Her Own Role and Style," *Chicago Tribune*, August 21, 1994, sec. 6, p. 5.

5. Carl M. Cannon, "Tipper," *Mother Jones*, January/February 1997, p. 26.

6. Buchholz, p. 5.

7. Tipper Gore, *Picture This: A Visual Diary* (New York: Broadway Books, 1996), p. 10.

8. Celia Dugger, "The Prime of Tipper Gore: Part Traditional Political Wife, Part Savvy Crusader, She's Ready to Play the Game," *The New York Times*, July 19, 1992, section 9, p. 9.

9. Sandra McElwaine, "Her Life, Her Love Story," *Good Housekeeping*, March 1993, p. 235.

10. Nancy Lloyd, "Tipper Gets Tough on TV, Curfews, Discipline," *Family Circle*, September 21, 1993, p. 46.

11. Gail McKnight, "Tipper Gore: The Vice President's First Lady," *Saturday Evening Post*, March–April 1993, p. 38.

Chapter 5. Battling the Record Industry

1. Steven Dougherty, "Parents vs. Rock," *People*, September 16, 1985, p. 46.

2. Andrea Pawlyna, "Stance on Rock Music Lyrics Echoes After Candidate's Wife," *Evening Sun*, February 5, 1988.

3. Lois Romano, "Tipper Gore, Playing Down the Rock War: The Candidate's Wife, Defying Protests and Defending Her Man," *Washington Post*, March 29, 1988, p. D8.

4. Bonnie Gangelhoff, "Tipper's Political Encore," *Houston Post*, September 2, 1992, pp. D4–5.

5. Tipper Gore, *Raising PG Kids in an X-Rated Society* (New York: Bantam Books, 1987), p. 2.

6. Carl M. Cannon, "Unsinkable Tipper Gore," *Baltimore Evening Sun*, June 20, 1994.

7. Irvin Molotsky, "On the Uses of Power by Marriage," *The New York Times*, September 29, 1985, p. 60.

8. Maureen Downey, "Flip Sides of the Record-labeling Question," *Atlanta Journal,* November 1, 1985.

9. Note to the author from Tipper Gore, March 13, 1998.

10. Gore, p. 19.

11. Jay Cocks, "Rock Is a Four-letter Word; a Senate Committee Asks: Have Lyrics Gone Too Far?" *Time,* September 30, 1985, p. 70.

12. Hendrick Hertzberg, "Tipper de doo dah," *New Republic,* December 7, 1987, p. 22.

13. James W. Brosnan, "Mrs. Gore's Advice to Parents Carries a Parental Advisory," *Memphis Commercial Appeal,* April 19, 1987.

14. Mike Bradley, "Tipper's Cause: As Husband Plans for Presidency, Gore Keeps Busy With Book, Talks," *Knoxville Journal,* April 14, 1987.

Chapter 6. A Hard Campaign

1. Sherrye Henry, "Talking to . . . Albert Gore, Jr.," *Vogue,* May 1988, p. 62.

2. "Tipper Gore Denies Reports of Shift on Lewd Rock Issue," *The New York Times,* November 7, 1987, p. 8.

3. Note to the author from Tipper Gore, March 13, 1998.

4. Karen DeWitt, "1985 Crusade by Tipper Gore Is Likely to Help 1992 Ticket," *The New York Times,* July 10, 1992, p. A17.

5. Lois Romano, "Tipper Gore, Playing down the Rock War: The Candidate's Wife, Defying Protests and Defending Her Man," *Washington Post,* March 29, 1988, p. D8.

6. Ibid.

7. Barbara Matusow, "Tipper's Revenge," *Washingtonian,* October 1994, p. 81.

Chapter 7. ". . . Everything Else Stopped"

1. "Gore's Son Stable After Accident," *Washington Post,* April 5, 1989, p. B3.

2. Marlene Cimons, "Tip-top Shape," *Runner's World*, June 1994, p. 46.

3. Claudia Glenn Dowling and David Burnett, "Keeping Track of Tipper," *Life*, March 1994, p. 82.

4. Elizabeth Gleick, "Tipper's Return," *People*, July 27, 1992, p. 34.

5. Barbara Matusow, "Tipper's Revenge," *Washingtonian*, October 1994, p. 79.

6. Celia Dugger, "Prime of Tipper Gore: Part Traditional Political Wife, Part Savvy Crusader, She's Ready to Play the Game," *The New York Times*, July 19, 1992, section 9, p. 1.

7. Marjorie Rosen, "Trimmer Tipper," *People*, August 2, 1993, p. 40.

8. Ibid.

9. Ibid.

10. Sandra McElwaine, "Her Life, Her Love Story," *Good Housekeeping*, March 1993, p. 236.

Chapter 8. The Campaign Trail

1. Alex S. Jones, "Al Gore's Double Life," *New York Times Magazine*, October 25, 1993, p. 42.

2. Rebecca Ferrar, "Let's Assist 'Real' Families, Says Tipper Gore," *Knoxville News Sentinel*, October 4, 1992.

3. Howard G. Chua-Eoan, "First Friends: Hillary Clinton and Tipper Gore Are Pals and Very Different Role Models," *People*, November 16, 1992, p. 92.

4. Kate McMullan, *Story of Bill Clinton and Al Gore, Our Nation's Leaders* (Milwaukee: Gareth Stevens Publishing, 1996), p. 78.

5. Barbara Matusow, "Tipper's Revenge," *Washingtonian*, October 1994, p. 140.

6. "Mystery Caller Stumps Gore," *Washington Post*, September 10, 1992, p. A14.

7. Ibid.

8. Carl M. Cannon, "Unsinkable Tipper Gore," *Baltimore Evening Sun*, June 20, 1994, p. F12.

9. Colin Greer, "I Know There Is Help," *Parade Magazine*, September 11, 1994, pp. 4–5.

10. Carl M. Cannon, "Tipper," *Mother Jones*, January/February 1997, p. 24.

11. Jacqueline Trescott, "The Women With a Ticket to Ride: Tipper Gore, Putting the Family First," *Washington Post*, July 16, 1992, p. C2.

12. Bill Hewitt, "Tennessee Waltz," *People*, November 16, 1992, p. 98.

13. Marian Burros, "Tipper Gore Wins a Campaign to Get Thin in Washington," *New York Times Biographical Service*, July 1993, p. 938.

Chapter 9. Second Lady

1. Marjorie Rosen, "Trimmer Tipper," *People*, August, 1993, p. 40.

2. Gail Kerr, "Gore Likes Life at Eye of the Storm: First Year Was Full of Changes, Work," *Nashville Tennessean*, January 23, 1994, p. C10.

3. Ibid.

4. Marilyn Achiron, "Making a Splash," *People*, August 16, 1993, p. 79.

5. Tipper Gore, *Picture This: A Visual Diary* (New York: Broadway Books, 1996), p. 15.

6. Barbara Matusow, "Tipper's Revenge," *Washingtonian*, October 1994, p. 140.

7. Joel Achenbach, "Tipper Gore. No, Seriously," *Washington Post*, May 16, 1993, p. F6.

8. Colin Greer, "I Know There Is Help," *Parade Magazine*, September 11, 1994, p. 7.

9. Ibid.

10. Claudia Glenn Dowling and David Burnett, "Keeping Track of Tipper," *Life*, March 1994, p. 82.

11. Pamela Warrick, "Tipper Gore's Mission of Mercy," *Los Angeles Times*, August 15, 1994, p. E1.

Chapter 10. *Picture This*

1. Eve Zibart, "Inside the Visual Diary of Tipper Gore," on the Internet at <www@bookpage.com>

2. Alexandra Jacobs, "Exposing Her Vice: Not for Tipper's Eyes Only," *Entertainment Weekly*, September 20, 1996, p. 73.

3. Michael Killian, " 'Second Lady': Look Behind the Scenes, and There's More Than Meets the Eye to Tipper Gore," *Chicago Tribune*, August 29, 1996, Section 5, p. 4.

4. Joel Achebach, "Tipper When Wet," *Washington Post*, August 27, 1996, p. B2.

5. Carl M. Cannon, "Tipper," *Mother Jones*, January/ February 1997, p. 28.

6. Claudia Glenn Dowling and David Burnett, "Keeping Track of Tipper," *Life*, March 1994, p. 82.

7. Ibid.

Further Reading

Cannon, Carl M. "Tipper." *Mother Jones*, January/February 1997, p. 22.

Conant, Jennet. "Family First." *Redbook*, March 1994, p. 80.

Dowling, Claudia Glenn, and David Burnett. "Keeping Track of Tipper." *Life*, March 1994, p. 82.

Gore, Tipper. *Picture This: A Visual Diary*. New York: Broadway Books, 1996.

Guernsey, JoAnn Bren. *Tipper Gore: Voice for the Voiceless*. Minneapolis: Lerner Publications Company, 1994.

Mansfield, Stephanie. "The Hipper Tipper." *Lear's*, April 1994, p. 52.

On the Internet

Tipper Gore's Website, with links to her speeches, "In-Focus" monthly column, and more

<http://www.whitehouse.gov/WH/EOP/VP_Wife/index.html> (September 15, 1998).

24 Hours in Cyberspace, Inc. "Picture This." Into the Light. 1996.

<http://www.cyber24.com/htm2/4_311.htm> (September 15, 1998).

Index